To read fluently is one of the basic aims of anyone learning English as a foreign language. **And it's never too early to start.** Ladybird Graded Readers are interesting but simple stories designed to encourage children between the ages of 6 and 10 to read with pleasure.

Reading is an excellent way of reinforcing language already acquired, as well as broadening a child's vocabulary. Ladybird Graded Readers use a limited number of grammatical structures and a carefully controlled vocabulary, but where the story demands it, a small number of words outside the basic vocabulary are introduced. In ***Town Mouse and Country Mouse*** the following words are outside the basic vocabulary for this grade:

carpet, cleaner, Christmas, climb, country, mouse, noisy, parcel, park

Further details of the structures and vocabulary used at each grade can be found in the Ladybird Graded Readers *leaflet.*

A list of books in the series can be found on the back cover.

British Library Cataloguing in Publication Data

Ullstein, Sue
Town Mouse and Country Mouse.—
(English language teaching).
1. English language—Text-books for foreign speakers
2. Readers—*1950-*
I. Title II. Dyke, John III. Aesop, Fables IV. Series
428.6'4 PE1128

ISBN 0-7214-1044-8

First edition

Published by Ladybird Books Ltd Loughborough Leicestershire UK
Ladybird Books Inc Lewiston Maine 04240 USA

Printed in England

Town Mouse and Country Mouse

written by Sue Ullstein
illustrated by John Dyke

Ladybird Books

This is Country Mouse. He lives in the country.

His home is in a
tree.

This is Town Mouse.
He lives in the town.

His home is in a house.

Town Mouse comes to the country. He wants to stay with Country Mouse.

Country Mouse says,
"I like the country.

It's quiet. You'll be happy here, Town Mouse."

This owl wants to catch Town Mouse and Country Mouse. They run away.

Country Mouse says,
"Come into this tree,
Town Mouse! Hurry! Hurry!"

Country Mouse and Town Mouse have supper.

Town Mouse says,
"I don't like this food.
It isn't like the food
in the town."

Country Mouse and
Town Mouse go to bed.

Town Mouse says,
"I don't like this bed.
It isn't like my bed
in the town."

Town Mouse tells Country Mouse, "It's too quiet here. I can't sleep!"

The next day Country Mouse is looking for food.

"Come and help me," he says.

"No," Town Mouse says.
"In the town we have
shops. We can buy
food."

Then Town Mouse sees some horses. He is afraid. He runs away.

He jumps into the water.

Town Mouse says,
"I don't like the country.
I want to go home.

We don't have horses in
the town."

"Come with me to the town, Country Mouse," Town Mouse says.

''We can go to the shops in the town.''

Town Mouse sees a car.

"Look," he says. "We can go to the town in this car."

They jump into the car.

The car goes to the town. Country Mouse sees the shops.

He sees the cars. It is not quiet in the town. It is noisy.

Town Mouse says,
"I like the town.
I don't live in a tree.
I live in a house.

You'll be happy here,
Country Mouse."

Town Mouse and Country Mouse have supper.

Country Mouse says,
"I don't like this food.
It isn't like the
food in the country."

Town Mouse and Country Mouse go to bed.

Country Mouse says,
"I don't like this
bed. It isn't like
my bed in the country."

Country Mouse tells Town Mouse, "It's too noisy here. I can't sleep."

The next day Town
Mouse and Country
Mouse go to the park.
They play with a ball.
They are happy.

Then Country Mouse sees a dog. The dog wants their ball. Country Mouse is afraid. He runs away. He jumps into the water.

Country Mouse sees a carpet cleaner in the house. He is afraid. He runs away again.

''Come into this hole,
Country Mouse!'' Town
Mouse says. ''Hurry!
Hurry!''

This cat wants to
catch Town Mouse and
Country Mouse. They
are in the hole.

Country Mouse says,
"I don't like the town.
I want to go home."

Country Mouse sees a
Christmas tree and
some Christmas parcels.

"Look," Town Mouse says.
"This parcel is going
to the country. It's
going near your home.
You can go home
inside the parcel."

The parcel is in a car. Country Mouse is inside the parcel.

The car goes to the country.

Country Mouse says,
"Here's my home. I'm
happy in the country.
I don't like the town.

I'm a country mouse
not a town mouse."